Introduction and Rondo Capriccioso

for Violin and Piano

CAMILLE SAINT-SAËNS Op. 28

Critical Urtext Edition

Edited by Endre Granat

FOREWORD

The *Introduction and Rondo Capriccioso* for Violin and Orchestra was originally intended to be the rousing Finale to Saint-Saëns' First Violin Concerto, op.20. The work was completed in 1863.

Saint-Saëns' favorite violinist Pablo de Sarasate gave the first performance in 1867 in Paris with the composer conducting. In 1869, Saint-Saëns entrusted his younger colleague Georges Bizet to create a reduction of the orchestra score for Violin and Piano. Claude Debussy, at Saint-Saëns' request transcribed the work for two pianos. The work is dedicated to Pablo de Sarasate. The composer's autograph score and the first edition of the work were our primary source material.

Endre Granat

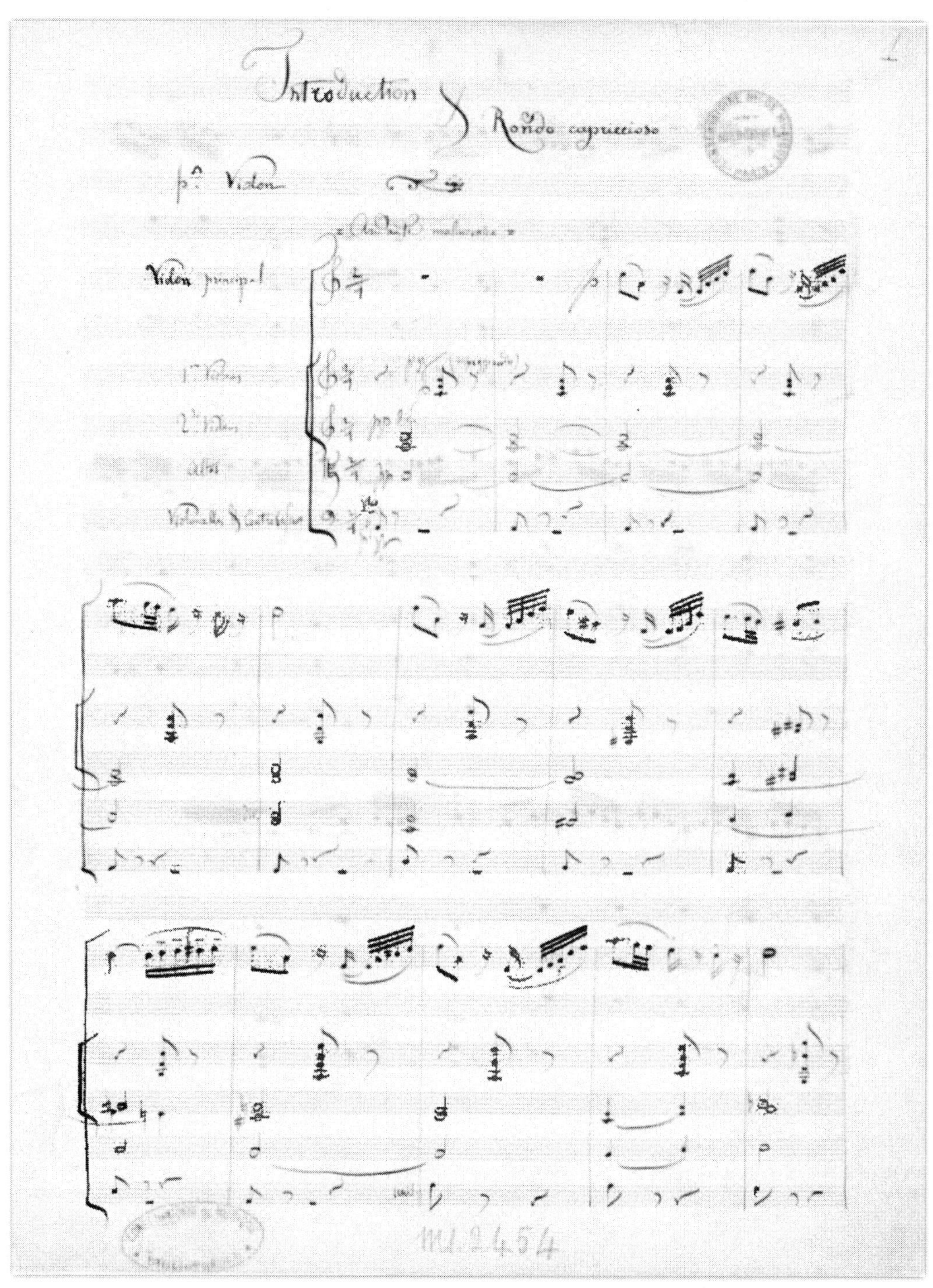

Camille Saint-Saëns Manuscript Fascimile
Introduction and Rondo Capriccioso
Courtesy of the Bibliothèque nationale de France

INTRODUCTION AND RONDO CAPRICCIOSO

for Violin and Piano

CAMILLE SAINT-SAËNS, Op. 28

20
sf
p
24
sf
tranquillo
ten.
ten.
pp
ppp
28
Viole & Bassi
32
marcato
Violin II
cresc. molto
f
A
37
Allegro ma non troppo.
p
Allegro ma non troppo. (♩.=88)
f TUTTI. Quatuor.
dim.

43
49
Cor.
55
61
67
pp
Quatuor

73
78
pp
83
Clar.
Fag.
88
f
Fl.
p
sf
Gor. & Fag.

92

fp

f

2 Fl.

sf

Ped.

95

Oboe

pp

98

Fag.

101

105
B
TUTTI.
Quatuor
109
115
Fl. & Clar.
Cor.
Oboe
legg.
121
cresc.
125
C
TUTTI

129
ten.
sf
sf
134
Oboe & Clar.
Fl. & Oboe
p
139
Clar.
143
Ob, Clar. & Cor.
147
dim.
dim.

151
p
con morbidezza
pp
Quatuor
155
159
163
167
poco - a - poco - cresc - -

INTRODUCTION and RONDO CAPRICCIOSO
for Violin and Piano

Violin

Critical Urtext Edition
Edited by Endre Granat

CAMILLE SAINT-SAËNS, Op. 28

* mm. 51 and 67: eighth note, eighth-note rest (Jascha Heifetz)

8va
(Jascha Heifetz)
1)
fp
f
2)
B
f
p
cresc.
f
8va
3)
C
7
1)
m. 93 in
autograph score
2)
m.103 in
autograph score
3)
mm. 126-127,
Jascha Heifetz

Con morbidezza
dim.
p
poco
a poco cresc.
f

* m. 199, fermata on the downbeat (Jascha Heifetz)

4) mm. 220-221, Jascha Heifetz

E
dim.
espr.
sf
leggiero
dolce
III
pp
IV
II
f
p

cresc.
F
dim.
cresc.
8va
cresc.
ad lib.
a tempo

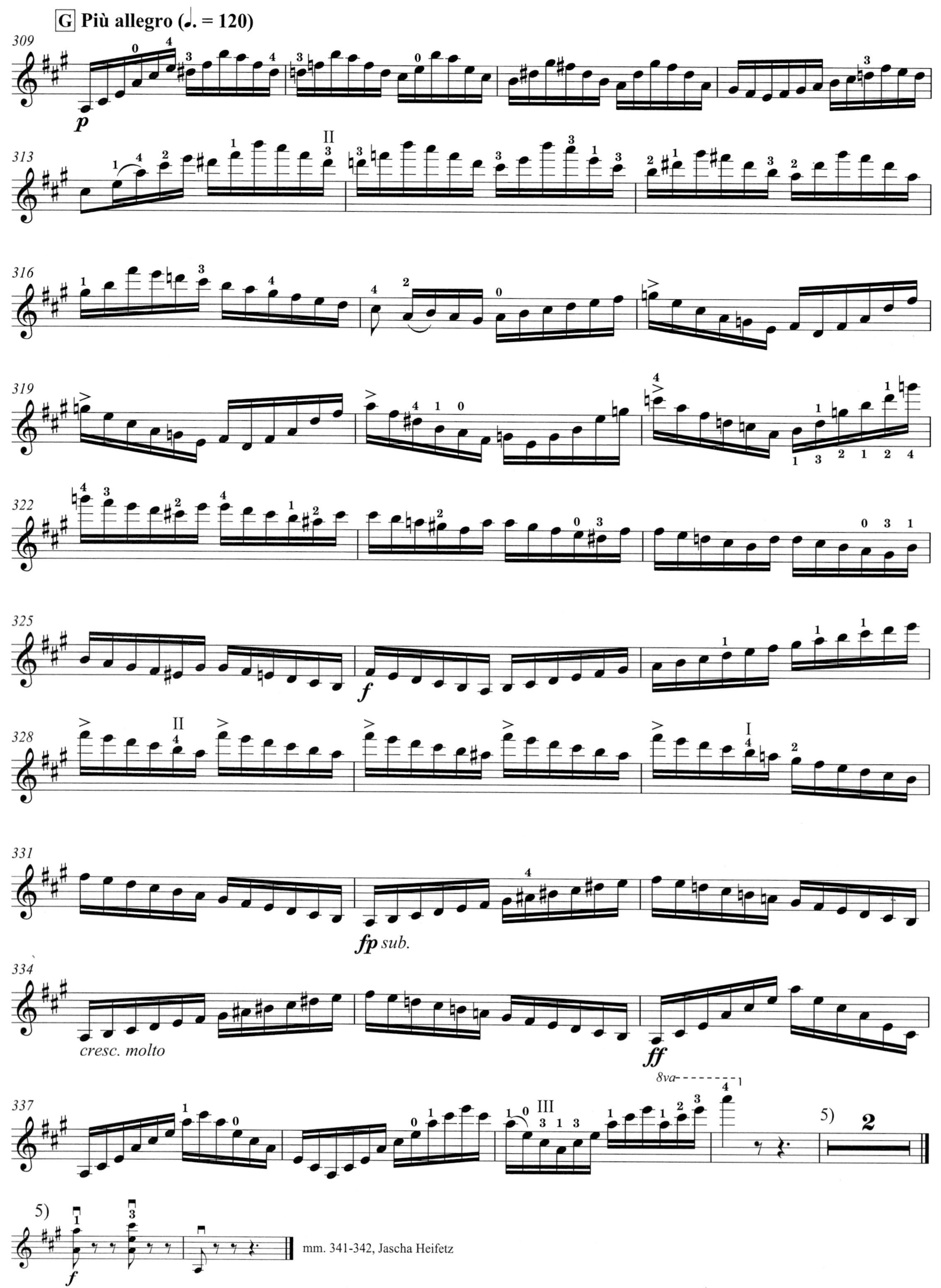
G Più allegro (♩. = 120)
p
II
f
II
I
fp sub.
cresc. molto
ff
8va
III
5)
2
5)
f
mm. 341-342, Jascha Heifetz

172
Clar.
177
poco cresc.
Fag.
181
f
Timp.
Cor. & Fag.
Timp.
185
dim.
p Fl. Ob. & Clar.
189
p
pp

194
8
198
D
f
sf
f TUTTI
p Quatuor
203
cresc.
209
cresc.
dim.
p
legg.

214
cresc.
f
219
8
rall.
f
ff TUTTI
ten.
224
sf
sf
229
E
f
p
p
Violin I
pp
Violin I
dim.

235
espressivo
sf
Cor. II
pp Quatuor
mf Clar.
p
241
sf
legg.
mf
p
Clar.
cresc.
248
dolce
dim.
pp
255
pp
leggierissimo
Quatuor

261
266
Cor. & Fag.
272
dim. p
Fl. & Oboe
276
cresc.

280
F
f
f
TUTTI
f
284
dim.
p
Oboe Solo
f brillante
p Quatuor pizz.
288
Fl. Solo
292
Oboe

296
cresc.
Clar.
Trump.
Fl.
300
p TUTTI
cresc.
303
ad lib.
ff
f
305
a tempo
Timp. Solo
f
dim.
sf
dim.
p

G
Più allegro.
Più allegro. (♩.=120)
Viole
Timb.
'Cello
Fl. & Oboe
fp
Quatuor

326
f
p Cor. & Fag.
f Trump.
330
Timp. p
f p subito
pp Quatuor
Oboe
334
cresc. molto
Fl. & Clar.
cresc.
ff
mf Timp. Solo
cresc.
338
8
f
TUTTI ff

NEW PUBLICATIONS FOR VIOLIN

The HEIFETZ *Collection*

We are pleased to introduce an exclusive series of Jascha Heifetz violin editions including wonderful and yet previously unpublished arrangements and transcriptions from Heifetz's own manuscripts.

G.F. HANDEL
PASSACAGLIA FOR TWO VIOLINS

Ed. Stephen Shipps/ Endre Granat Outside of his native Norway, Johan Halvorsen (1864-1935) is known internationally only for his arrangement of Handel's Harpsichord Suite. The Passacaglia is performed as a mainstay of Duo programs in his arrangements for both Violin/Viola and Violin/ Cello. Jascha Heifetz established these duos in the standard literature by playing and recording countless performances with William Primrose and Gregor Piatigorsky. HL00126549—S512002 .... $22.95

CAMILLE SAINT-SAËNS
HAVANAISE FOR VIOLIN AND PIANO

Ed. Endre Granat. The Havanaise (Habanera in French) by Camille Saint-Saëns op.83 dates from 1885-87. The composer dedicated this work to Rafael Diaz Albertini, a violinist of Cuban origin. In 1888 Saint-Saëns completed the orchestration of the Havanaise . This Critical Urtext Edition is based on the composer's manuscript, the first print of the violin and piano version, and to a large part, on the historic recording by the composer himself with the violinist Gabriel Willaume (1919). HL00141932—S511022 .... $14.95

CAMILLE SAINT-SAËNS
INTRODUCTION AND RONDO CAPRICCIOSO OP. 28, CRITICAL URTEXT EDITION

Ed. Endre Granat. The Introduction and Rondo Capriccioso for Violin and Orchestra was originally intended to be the rousing Finale to Saint-Saëns' First Violin Concerto, op.20. Saint-Saëns' favorite violinist Pablo de Sarasate gave the first performance in 1867 in Paris with the Composer conducting. In 1869 Saint-Saëns entrusted his younger colleague Georges Bizet to create a reduction of the orchestra score for Violin and Piano. The composer's autograph score and the first edition of the work were the primary source material for this publication.
HL00141931—S511021 .... $14.95

HENRYK WIENIAWSKI
POLONAISE BRILLANTE NO. 1 (Polonaise de Concert)

Ed. Endre Granat. In 1848, the thirteen year old Henryk Wieniawski wrote the first sketches to his Polonaise in D major. Tremendously popular already during the composer's life time, this work has been on the repertory of virtually every virtuoso violinist ever since. This new Critical Urtext Edition corrects obvious misprints while keeping the format of the 1853 first edition, incorporating the textural the later Paris version as foot notes.
HL00141930—S511020 .... $12.95

HENRYK WIENIAWSKI
POLONAISE BRILLANTE NO. 2

Ed. Endre Granat. Henryk Wieniawski completed his Polonaise No. 2 at the zenith of his career in 1869. This virtuoso piece showcases the playing of many fast, short and accented notes on one bow stroke, called the Wieniawski staccato, whilte the slow midsection in F major contains some of his most lyrical themes.
HL00126550—S511019 .... $14.95

CONTEMPORARY SOLOS *Original works & transcriptions*

J.S. BACH—TOCCATA AND FUGUE IN D MINOR FOR SOLO VIOLIN

Arr. Stuart Carlson. Intrigued by the fact that many of the chords and motifs within Bach's famous *Toccata and Fugue* for organ could be adapted for the violin, competition-winning soloist Stuart Carlson created this virtuosic arrangement. It is in the piece's original key, and it is designed to convey the full and grand sound of the organ to the solo violin. This arrangement intentionally creates the true sound of Bach's piece, while adding variation-like figures within the Fugue's main theme. HL00124287—S510009 .... $11.95

STEPHEN HARTKE—NETSUKE FOR VIOLIN & PIANO

Netsuke are Japanese miniature carvings that were originally made to secure objects suspended from a man's sash. This piece was inspired by six exquisite carvings from the Bushell Collection at the Los Angeles County Museum of Art.
HL00042670—X511045 .... $37.95

YEVHEN STANKOVYCH—ANGELS' TOUCH FOR VIOLIN & PIANO

When recounting the premiere performance of *Angels' Touch,* violinist Solomiya Ivakhiv describes a work which "embodies a child-like mysticism, exploring naivety, hope, and inner peace leading to enlightenment. It is sprinkled with Ukrainian folklore elements from the Carpathian Mountains, also reminding me of my own childhood." HL00127941—S511018 .... $12.95

YEVHEN STANKOVYCH—CONCERTO NO. 2 FOR VIOLIN AND ORCHESTRA—SOLO/ PIANO REDUCTION

This is the first print edition of celebrated composer Yevhen Stankovych's second violin concerto, featuring cadenzas, fingerings and bowings by violinist Dima Tkachenko. Duration ca. 24' HL00141939—S511023 .... $24.95

Prices subject to change without notice.